CW00454925

:an UNFINISHED dance:

Jim Ferguson

to
JAMES KELMAN
for inspiration
and a desk
on which
to write

:an UNFINISHED dance:

ane autobiography of everyone

being a long poem in four parts
on politics, literature, life
with notes

written in the period
1st April to 30th June 2020
aka 'covid 19 lockdown # 1'

Jim Ferguson

with a preface by
RUBY MCCANN

First published 2022
by Rymour Books
45 Needless Road
PERTH
PH2 0LE

https://www.rymour.co.uk

© Jim Ferguson 2021

ISBN 978-1-7398466-9-5

Cover design by Ian Spring
Printed and bound by
Imprint Digital
Seychelles Farm
Upton Pyne
Exeter

Jim Ferguson is hereby identified as the author of this work in accordance with Section 77 of the Copyright, Design and Patents Act 1988

All rights reserved. No part of this publication may be reproduced, stored in a retrieval system, or transmitted, in any form or by any means, electronic, mechanical, photocopying, recording or otherwise, without the prior permission of the publishers.

The paper used in this book is approved
by the Forest Stewardship Council
FSC

PREFACE

A hybrid stream of consciousness narrative poem, *An Unfinished Dance* by Jim Ferguson is entertaining, thought-provoking and witty with mortality as the underlying theme relayed by an unreliable though persistent narrator. (*Or*, is it really 'just a bunch of dead people/talking to each other?')

Death permeates this long four-part poem, from dead family to dead friends, to dead poets, and writers—all raging against the system. It is a unique look into the intimate landscape of the mind that gives shape to the façade that for the working classes, the ordinary man (or woman) the dance never ends. And it's a dance with death!

Genuinely experimental, Jim Ferguson forces us to see the world differently—like 'a thought/that accidently/lands in your/head.' The constantly changing language feeds eerie imaginings in various tongues (reflected in the use of various fonts): English, Glaswegian, Scots, and French. It is darkly comic, a manual for the dead written during the covid pandemic, it offers more than a hint of contained fury and anxiety, of empathy without sentimentality. A remarkable tale told by a voice that's utterly compelling and which you read with the feeling that you're being led inside the murkiest of minds. No one is in control of these irresistible and disturbing musings.

If you love poetry, you'll love this book. Proof that we can still engage with stimulating ideas: 'let the language carry you/ float on the weight of the words.'

Ruby McCann

ACKNOWLEDGEMENTS

Extracts from this poem have been published in *Cerasus* magazine. Thanks to Louise Malone and Ian Spring for the cover design.

part 1. A Sun God Awake at the Wheel

who on earth
could ever perform
such a dance as this?

_____

although always

love n wonder

always always
never never

signing up for peace

carrying a bigger stick ●

Our Father
        Who art buried
                Somewhere down
Morecambe way

not really too far
from the Blackpool tower—
a giant sideways smile
with millions of teeth
and yet many missing

under the sands those small worms
under the water ashes and bodies
migrant workers
drowned in the bay[1]

_____

west ◀━━━━━━━━▶ east

_____

oral bacteria
bugs in your mouth
live on your gums
crawl in the spaces
between your teeth

flossing is murder

hence

carbolic soap for dangerous words

jim ferguson

the truncation of
clichés

idiomatic speech patterns on the page
ballet dancers in the clouds
as likely as
magic dust
abracadabra
smoke n mirrors

only men allowed
in the magic circle
or
women who are laddettes

tragic

sit doon, relax, smoke a
cigarette,

try doing an unfinished dance
_____

north

↑

↓

south

_____

a smattrin uv Scots   *soo pehr bbb*

a smehtttehring of Scots *trendy iz fuck*

talking is not touching
smoke cannot read

crosses several boundaries
sex, class, race, nation

a little like the wind
which is welcome when gentle

very subtly cut down to size
it's preferable to *them*

for *us* all to remain
inside the stereotype. so   …

_____

north east

south west

_____

I knew it all along
sense of impending death

call it a syndrome related to anxiety
or
doom

jim ferguson

christ, he's another yin,
a syndrome aboot death related to anxiety
ergo christ is anxiety and death

———————————

cheery bastards everywhere
know alls watchin the boxin
sport of kings
something to jest aboot

am a miserable-ists miserable-ist
miserablism just pours oot mi
fucksake eh

am nuclear powered
good for the ozone
bad for the soil
bad for the species
bad for the future

smoke emerges frae giant chimneys
ye kin see for miles   look

looks quite b. b. b. beautiful
fuckin miserable ya beauty

———————————————

north west

south west

———————————————

livn on a windfarm
fresh air fortnight

health effects
lead to

longer life

_____

U.H.T. Breast Milk

radioactive nipples

I
am
the personal pronoun
which therefore
thinks

not

who says that
it wisny me

any questions?

QUESTION: Why does an occupying army call the
citizens of the occupied country 'foreigners'?

ANSWER: The nation state is a dead duck except when
required to justify the expansion of global markets.

jim ferguson

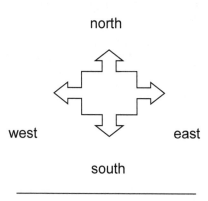

north

west   east

south

**the concept of *the*
'national interest'**

Later you are thinking

that's the origin of love
not biology at all —

forget Darwin[2]
    dead revolutionary
        crazy insurgent

marrying strictly
    inside the tribe
        never outside

old fathers
    and older grandfathers
        see to it

jim ferguson

who sings sweet georgia brown
who is a tribalist-racist
                in this town?

who thinks the old   are the wiser? now

———

from zero to two in one easy step
havent you had enough yet

———

you cant take
emotional lumps

from other people

still expect love
to walk through the door

without scabs and bruises

damaged hearts
the only things

you left behind

———

of course not,
i dont know who you are

dont know who is writing who
havent you had enough yet   no?

jim ferguson

fonts in conversation
talking to each other on the same page

without anyones permission
where is the authorial control here?

i demand to know who is in charge! exclaimed the italics

i demand to know who is in authority!

The Onomatopoeia of Empty Vessels

A definition of President Trump[3]
— The Onomatopoeia of an Empty Vessel

— No, a gangster.

canny be right that
canny be

some cunt's
made a fuck up

here

here you

did you jist fuck-up there

it wiz yu winnit
ah know it fukn wiz

bastard

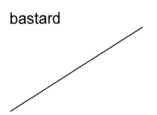

whers ma tabacca
where ye left it

ach
ya fucker
we're dead

we were dead
from the beginning
imagine

only money mattered
that and turning out the vote
the right way round

labour philistines
didn't give a shit
about art or politics

they lined
their pockets
with power

leafy suburbs
and
second homes

laborious they were

jim ferguson

always in attendance
at interminable meetings

devoid of
everything visceral
that's how

they lost their Scottish
power-base
language was always

proper ing-lish
and references always
to workingclass roots

that made them cringe
in private
and in public too

they ridiculed their
cringing
littleselves

took NATO jobs[4]
invented acronyms
for atom bombs

so they could buy them //got a comfy chair at the United Nations
and promise 'the vote' //an amorphous mass too dumb to think
they'd never be used //a vanity project for the Rule Britannias

in effect useless //the American cousins the one true ally
useless in effect //it was always their finger on the button
dead from the neck //ULTIMATELY

jim ferguson   –17–

up
we were
of course

dead
we were dead
from the beginning

imagine.[5]

I was relentlessly happy

a happy lassie was I
relentlessly happy
a real happy lassie

relentlessy happy was I

there's no disguising
the pain in the arse
that i was

relentless cheerfulness
can get on
other peoples'

nerves

Big Time

Big Time
Thrives
Relentlessly

jim ferguson

Since the big-bang

In the company
Of Astro-physicists
Sightseers
Sooth-sayers

Descendents of Galileo[6]
And Nostradumus[7]
Strange inventors
Who work

With Number Theory
Algo-(i'll go)-rhythms
Hitherto Undiscovered Equations

That might
> *slip through*
>> *the cracks inspacetime*

Where they inhabit
Hitherto
Undiscovered

Space(s) – Ball(s) – Planet(s)

knowing you,
nothing is good

the wise ones
recognise this

but oh Pablo
I wish you'd left it
                    like that

and left a bit of breathing space,
an escape into the light, towards
the liberation of humans unknown

your mind is a different universe
pick-axe-joe

Who held most honorary degrees in Fine Arts,
                    Stalin or Picasso?

Damn, you're so 20th century,
pick-axe-joe

sounds like Picasso
describing Stalin

Brecht was terrified of Stalin, you know
You know you shouldn't say that Pablo

Brecht was invincible
Stalin's brain was Swiss Cheese[8]

And appeared in Mother's Porridge
As a dumb-ass child and his sister

Was actually dumb
As in 'could not speak'

Who is talking to who?
I
am
talking
to
you

jim ferguson

You, talking to me[9] ... doesn't that sound over familiar

Rilke[10] was asking
after you

wondered about the status
of the Scottish parliament

if it was truly independent,
founded on a healthy kind of

love of humanity, or still
just money-lenders

outside the temple
pissing on miniature

angels they call ants—

Rilke asked, 'what is the guiding principle,
de-humanisation or to become the image of angels?'

Am I listening?

me
here

I hear you there

still one perfectly functional ear

it has an angel-horn

to be used in times of emergency

restore the earth to insurgency or

Elysian fields

pastoral paradise(s)

plural of paradise
                    paradii, perhaps not
aye
ah kin hear ye

turn that fuckin phone aff

ah don't even own
a mobile device

or even an IED[11]

Guido Fawkes[12] had an IED
but the barrels of gunpowder
were difficult to conceal

as was the plot itself
due the presence of
agent provocateurs

you could lose your head
with such shocking news
— I am not a muse, don't paint me

into a corner
I never would
'consider the situation'[13]

of such a possibility arising
who
is *saying ... this*

jim ferguson

that?

what?

not that!

I demand to know who is in authority.

where's the red wine for fuck's sake?

which do you prefer
ploughman's lunch
or
draftsman's sandwich?

i don't know what that latter is

A snack invented by René Daumal[14]
and Rab Zoso McLean[15]
of Hunterhill in the Scottish town of Paisley

*i don't know who Rab Zoso McLean of Hunterhill
is*

he invented The Draftsman's Sandwich, had
harpsichordal fingers, was a devotee of Future
Jazz

which music lies still
undiscovered, even by...

even by Astro-physicists
Sightseers
Sooth-sayers

Descendents of Galileo
And Nostradumus

jim ferguson   -23-

Strange inventors
Who work

With Number Theory
Algorithms and/or
Hitherto Undiscovered Equations

that's almost repetition
but you didn't say "*and/or*" before

didn't i, i meant to
must have been

a miscalculation
must have been.

Thinking time is necessary.
The unpaid labours of the brain

mighty gargantuan they are too. too
difficult for mere mortals

but easy for those who live and love
daily within the infinite, passé(d) on over

to the hotel with a different room
to sleep in forever every night

unending. unedifyingly
relentlessly happy in infinity

I know it.
Where the angel Rilke plays ping-pong
with Gurdjieff and other 'Serious Drinkers'[16]

such as Rab Zoso McLean of harpsichordal fame
Rene Daumal and believe it or not, Franz Kafka[17]

jim ferguson

Kafka, fuck me
Fuck me, kafka, yes the very man

It's a very male place
It's a hinterland

An analogue and a silhouette.

Not those
Neither of those

what, none of the above
Neither nor none of those above, indeed

Agreed
Agreed

Rilke expresses concern
that the Scottish Parliament be not
founded upon a greed agenda

AN agenda of greed?

agreed
a greed

agenda, you're playing silly games
wherein the hopeths (hope – eths)
of democracy doth ...
reside

Indeed reside.

indeed
indeed

motion carried
by beings diabolical
into the chamber
of the mother, father, sister, brother
of parliaments
the rose by any other

NOMECLATURA![18]

agreed indeed
indeed *a greed*

—————

My robotic PA, Deep Throat, (so named as its programming
has given it an infinite thirst for knowledge and inquiry into the
human understanding) asked me two questions this morning.
1. Can heterosexuals be heterophobes?
and
2. In the light of very recent history can Lady MacBeth's
compulsive Hand Washing be considered a positive human
attribute?

Ah, this is where robotics can help fend off dementia, I told Deep
Throat.

I'm confused, replied DT.

—————

i was suddenly awake
at the wheel

all that time wading through treacle

life had been dead
alive yes, but only just

authority was always

jim ferguson

always on my back

the system
on my mind

the money
in my mind

somehow there was never
never any freedom to speak of

always making
always doing

always always
surviving

waiting for this day
day of realisation

no longer
'a bought behaviour pattern'[19]

oh yes, it's great when you quote
from other poets

who said that?

ah, confused looking baby asleep,
you don't know, do you?

it was tom leonard, said that,
his name was tom

dead now, of course
of course

unlike this living self
with eyes de-scaled

seeing the world
as a child might

might cross the road without looking?

certainly not, not now
not that

though it's much the same process
the death of a child always

always has so much more impact
life is short

nasty, brutish business
they say, who said that?

some other dead fucker[20]
we live off the achievements of

the dead,
dead, yes always

always always
the dead

so

so
what will you do with your waking moments
bright eyes?

_____

jim ferguson

you don't know
what's in there do you

how would i
i haven't looked

even had you looked
you wouldn't know

i'd guess it's a corpse

you'd be wrong

looks like that sort of box

a corpse box,
a box made of corpses
what sick mind
would make such a thing?

i still say it looks like a coffin

They all say that

who do?

all of the uninformed
the bloated
the uniformly stupid

those who take comfort
in their old dead routines

those who take comfort
yes—
in their old dead terrines

jim ferguson   -29-

that meant to be funny
anti-french jokes
is that how low you are now

you're getting warmer

is it ashes?

no

i've looked in
it looks like ashes

its the dead dust
of five hundred
heads of garlic

pardon

it's the...

I heard you

dead dust
of five hundred
heads of garlic

must you say that

thought you'd want to know

i didn't want to know
i'd looked in already
looked in when you weren't looking

going behind my back now

jim ferguson

i didn't go anywhere
i just looked in,
it's a curious box
—looks like a coffin

it's a tourrine

there's no such thing

it is anyway

if you don't watch out
Ronnie Laing[21] will come
and you take away

away, away where?

the nut house
crazy palace
booby hatch

asylum?

there's never that
never any kind of asylum
one scoffs at such

feeble mindedness

no, not now
wouldn't be

wouldn't be...

in keeping
not the done

thing

precisely

i'd have to doubt
that you doubt
the existence of angels

Davy Hume.[22]

———————

This dream unsettled me. Calling it was, there was a calling out. A scream or a moan or something in between. A yell. Aye, that would be it, a yell. It called out for a change of font. All this back and forth, two voices in the one head ever so confusing. Lacking in focus. Can ye hear me? Are ye there? Yous two. You two fuckin bastards. Where are ye? Off and deserted me, eh. Is that it? I awoke from a deep sleep, dreaming badly, crying out. I could hear myself crying out but could do nothing about it. I was being buried alive. It's a nightmare really, not just a bad dream. There was someone talking. A nagging voice, a nagging man's voice, and a young man at that. Perplexing. Incongruous. Oxymoronic. That's the kind of word you want to be using, so it is. Wake up from a nighmare only to be in another nightmare but the other nightmare is actual fucking reality. Aye, that's what reality is, yer actual fucking reality. And your actual reality is depressing. It's a depressing fuckin monologue. I mean, that's where you live. Your entire fucking existence— there's no more than one voice. Aw the other voices are dead and you're dead inside too. There's nobody. Nobody awake at the wheel, no one driving. You're a driverless car, a rudderless ship. There's nae big brother or sister to help. Nae maw and da. I mean every cunt's deid. That's fuckin it. That's it I mean. Platitude after platitudes. Total.

jim ferguson

There's no point in worrying about that. That was the old you. This is the new you. A brand new you. Shiny, of course. Made of plastic, of course. You like yoga, yoghurt and high bran foods. You're verging on vegan. Still like the odd drop of coo's juice but you know you're trying. You're making a difference. The planet Earth greets you each morning into its welcoming arms. You love the planet Earth. The planet Earth loves you right back. It loves your mindfulness and meditative moods. It loves the car in your garage and the walk you take to the bottle bank. The planet Earth loves you so much it gives of its resources freely so that you can binge on them until you and rest of your species perish. The planet Earth loves you so much it gives just like God gave Jesus the son. So that Christianity could spread like a virus and wipe everything out. Go on ya cunt, oot the road. Make way for a different species at the top of the food chain. A different species can make a difference. A brand new species. A brand new difference. Shiny. Plastic. A revolution in evolution. Cataclysmic. Yes that's the kind of word you want to be using. Cataclysmic! So much better than 'oxymoronic', Jesus, that's the fucking rain on. You won't even be going out for a walk now. Nobody talks anyway. The only voices you notice are them inside your head. You know who they are. Mental.

---

there's Dostoevsky's **Bobok**[23]
of course

what's that?

just a bunch of dead people
talking to each other

that's nice
just like us

only they don't get on

and we do?

they're all cooped up
together
underground, in coffins,
there's no escape

exactly like us then

aye mibbe

no, exactly

Philosopher and literary critic Mikhail Bakhtin
regarded it as a fine work.[24]

yeah they
shoot each other
pwew pwew
with imaginary guns

like when you were young
and overdosed on cowboy movies
John Wayne[25] made you happy
though IRL he was very fright-wing

rightening but never
even sniffed a war
he knew the USA
that way President Trump knows his Hitler

ah yes
the totalitarian shaman
him with (or without) the 'bad moustache'

jim ferguson

mother always said
'you could tell a lot
from the grooming of his face'

while taking a bath
with Herbert Marcuse[26]
i was surprised that

facial moisturising man
'one dimensional man'
and
"all in this together" man

are
in fact
all
one and the same

man
or woman
agreed

women are
all too often
often excluded

you're liberal
about whom
you bathe with

(with whom you bath)

and liberal too
about who
i shave with

(let me too)

tell you
inside this system
of grooming

alienation is
universal
our owners

often have
similar tastes
to likes of us

we're all happily objectified
de Beauvoir was Sartre's[27]
quill-dip-appendage for...

of course we are
all happily objectified
and equal at the point of consumption

(?) *i'd question that*
you have to have the money
I have to have the money?

the real political debates
take place in the divorce courts
and in bedrooms

yes of course
in bedrooms of course   *in bedrooms of course*

a 'bad moustache' is no laughing matter
unless you're Woody Allen[28]
yes of course

and where is Dostoevsky in all this?

jim ferguson

at rest in his grave
awaiting The Redemption
and an end to humanity's corruption

he'll be there a while
yes, mother always said,
'you're a long time deid'

or dead

dead always
always *always*

the dead

———————

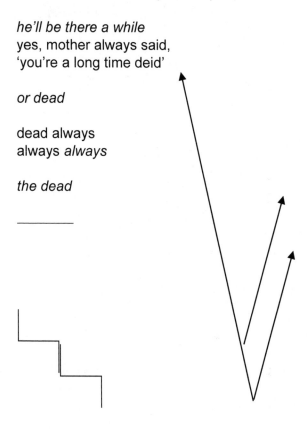

bags
of
dogshit
hang from trees

in pet cemeteries
where
our pets remain
unburied

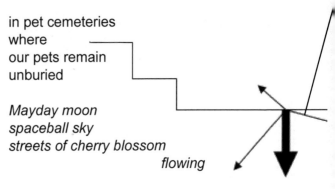

Mayday moon
spaceball sky
streets of cherry blossom
                    flowing

mother-nature pacifies
the struggle
for the meaning
of existence

as mother always said
'when humankind are so unkind
makes folks wish folk dead'

I loved
it
when she talked American-a-*a-*

―――――

lways, me too ■   *sun-filled eyes*

                        beautiful vision
                        brand new world

truly
comical concerns
cash or card?
unmatched stockings

jim ferguson

red beret or pillbox hat?
                    glowing

the very best thing
that glows in the dark
is our summer sun
but does not know it

_____

_____

not quite so deeply
inside the self

at a space
in there

where pacification
of a certain kind arises

you are the self inside the self
like an acorn hidden in a haystack

still you remain unsure of your number—
same number for 14 years

but you cant quite recall it now
14 years have passed

and this old familiar
telephone number is

no longer
familiar
but not being so deep
inside the self

it does not trouble

jim ferguson

that
the exact location

of the thought process
remains unknown

you know its somewhere
indside the head

but just which number
to key in exactly

to find the location
is woolly. Passion,

reduced but present,
can help and later

you wont feel
a thing. know

a thing. be
a thing.

yet in truth a thing is exactly what you
will be
when you cease to be a person, who said
that?

who?

You placed a picture on the clipboard.
What is it doing there? It is a map
of the progress made in this society
of disappointments over the years .

and strange how peaceful

jim ferguson

the tumult has become

all and everything
ever so strange

final calm resolution
of *The Glass Bead Game*[29]

———————

———————

there is no double underline
beneath the soul   of course

of course it's bright, the sun's a star
source of light and life, why not call it god
indeed why not?

part 2. No Profit in Prophets

at home with goddard[30]
contemplating the place

of art in human life
all we ever watch is

goddard, no sports
or game shows

or 24 hour news—
is art all about the work?

travailler: 'remember,
its about the work, Jim.'[31]

is it always the work
and never the money

always production
and never consumption?

travailler

travail
travailler

travail

*the terror within Reason[32]
sits on Henry Ford's knees
like an automatic rifle*
artists are irrelevant,
sit quiet, take the money
say nothing

jim ferguson

others starve or self-destruct
or dishonest poverty
eats them for breakfast

saying something
muttering incoherently
but never never

on tv
they're writing essays
on Mickey Rourke's Face[33]

but all the words
slide off
Hollywood celebrity

died with Brando[34]
super-charged image
of a superman

they wrote too many essays
on his face too
and it collapsed

beneath the weight
of its wealth and power
nice work if you can get it

bet on it!

many would say
on their six mile walk
for water today

a tv stunt for charity is
advertising waste
built into the fabric

of a system
that's corrupt
a mammoth construction

from men who like walls
let us in, let us out
on a whim

they're making B-movies
out of Mickey Rourke's Face
such a talented waste

of resources
in the whoredom
of private jets

.

while the idiots
all fly economy

.

you take a missile
in and out
of the Gaza strip

but you cant
just simply
walk there

WTF

what the fuck
right enough
in genes

and in jeans
self perpetuating
myths

jim ferguson

in dreams
in dreams
in dreams

of empty lives
so shrivelled
there's nothing but hate

all the politics
in America
are the politics of race

'dont buy bullets'
i heard Alex Harvey say
dreaming an impossible dream

bigotry is easy
when your white big brother
doesnt jail you right aways

the terror inside Reason
sits on Henry Ford's knees
like an automatic rifle

————————
————————

cool spring morn
in April

1807

cobbler John Struthers[35]
poet John Struthers
historian John Struthers
singer John Struthers

is searching for the starting
point of Scottish music and song

deep within his handy work
it's a tortured journey inventing

and discovering the hidden
root of history of history

which requires very special
eyes to see, just back in January

Struthers was busy back in Paisley
got the coach at the halfway

and met his friend the

weaver Robert Tannahill[36]
poet Robert Tannahill
flautist Robert Tannahill
songwriter Robert Tannahill

the air sang with larks
as Struthers passed through

the village of Govan

well on his way
to the halfway

his walking boots strong
he'd made them himself

and the war was good for business
all those soldiers needed lasting souls

on their feet

jim ferguson

for dancing, for walking

for marching unto death
on Carunna's bloody shore

twas a source ironically
of certain men's felicity

but not
not for Tannahill

the war
it always reeked of blood

and death
    DEATH
        DEATH

— like an automatic rifle
WE were at a table typing

on Montgomery Street
Edinburgh in 2003

trying to make sense
of the death of Jimmy Toner

so sad to see him go
an overdose of pills or something

accidental little did
i know that 16 years later
you'd go the same way
Graham Brodie—[37]

little did you know

little did i know

little do you know
little do i know

and little will we know
when its all wrapped up

it's too early for wooden overcoat
we shout

of course it all makes sense
when there's no such thing as death

when you're there you don't know about
any other single simple thing

you can, can-can dance
you can operatic sing

but you're a disembodied thing
desublimated ... gone ...

we sat across the kitchen table
drank red wine and tried to write

Gibson kindly came along with hash

—but our writing was pure shite
and we couldn't make sense

of the death of Jimmy Toner
and we could do no justice
to his life

alas, poet Graham Brodie
we did try, explorer Graham Brodie

jim ferguson

all came to fuck all, publisher Graham Brodie
though are a good few books and some cds

beyond the village green
and left a bit
the source of Scottish music
the source of Scottish lyrics

indeed the very source of Scottish song
remains where it remains

and stays where it's always been
embedded in the origins

of the all human monkeys
somewhere on the continent

of Africa, of whom we are all,
the daughters and the sons

but does it really matter
who was in your family

200,000 (two hundred thousand)
years ago.

no no no, and humanity's true worth
if it has any worth at all

can surely only lie in making futures
unseen, in a dream beyond a dream

in transcending unnecessary
suffering and despair

in an LSD trance
when time has ceased to be

and the only thing we have
is ecstacy

d
d

don't try this at home
if you don't want to die
in an accidental overdose
of painless pain deferred

fossils tell us everything and nothing
fossils are fake news now
fossils tell us nothing new

science tells us everything and nothing
science is fake news now
science tells us nothing new

don't be fucking daft
be stupid
don't be fucking daft
be happy in our ignorance

learn to love the darkness
Darth Vader[38] is no accident
he is bringing peace at last
just like jesus

beyond the village green
you want to be philosophy
poetry aint enough

facial lines communicate
harm's done
by social isolation

jim ferguson

gangsters in the White House
think that they are legend
in the sick myths of their minds

want to
make martyrs of us all
difficult to tell

just who is fooling you
as one automatic rifle
metes out carnage in the mall

automatic Reason
a reflection of the prejudice within
the cruellest heart—

The Clash[39]
come tumbling
down the stairs

blasting 'Combat Rock'
everything that's digital
powered by electricity

neurones fire
electrons wander
making memories

making thought

and ideas
can live and love
quite happily
in books
in books
in paintings and in books

spiritual storage
spiritual reproduction—
is every extinction

a step nearer to an ending
or creation of a space
for something new?

the future now
the past apart
time's vertiginous flow

on we go
go on
do we?

there's frog spawn
and dynamite
colloids and suspensions

different DNAs
with every passing second
bad science that spells extinction

like cephalaspic fish
swim
across the universe

as beeps of radiation
pulse in packets of energy
smeared in thumb prints

and The Clash
are chasing
'Police and Thieves'

copyright free

jim ferguson

unpatented processes
walking on sunshine

photosynthesis
does the trick
over and over

and over
again
our magical

mysterious
mind numbing friend
from nowhere

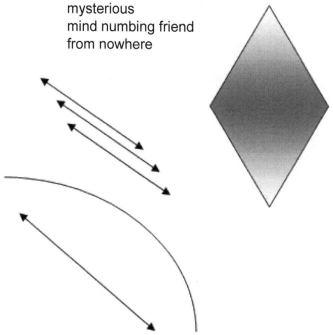

**if you had bright beads and lights to show the way
or lasers or electron beams
cabbages and onion rings
or bells and whistles
or a shiny rocket painted green
photochemical energy in infinite supply
you can travel anywhere**

jim ferguson

**always die before you get there,   ALWAYS   ALWAYS
                                        NEVER   NEVER**

**happy mister   see them   tap-dance on the clouds
under the eyes of endless blue skies,
she is always watching**
never gone   never out of reach by app or phone

This is advertising for Post-lockdown, Post-Brexit Lifestyle Inc.

Sponsored by @Trump Chickens International
"When I go to my local swimming baths, I always stuff a dead chicken down my trunks
before I dive in! That way when I bring it back home, cook it and eat it, I know the chicken
I'm eating is chlorine clean. And British too!"

mysterious
quantities

down amongst
uncertainties

so tiny
to us

they
can't be
untrue
let the language carry you
float on the weight of the words

Mintman Newton[40]

                                                    jim ferguson

is no use here

cause and effect
are one and the same

Rationalism's rifles
got jammed here

down amongst
uncertainties

so tiny
to us

they
can't be

untrue

you can be
two places at once

mysterious
quanta!

just a
bewtiful day

aye, n
wirraw alive

alive indeed
aye
——————

mysterious
quanta!

jim ferguson   –55–

in search of pleasure
just what are you looking for

eternal youth
the ocean

revolution
fruit in a bowl

control

is control a dirty word
or can you take it back

feel control
feel in control

be control
surf it fast

hold the chaos
channel control

when control
is what you need

Take back control[41]
Control the virus

control your life
control your health

control the aging process
you will be uncle bob[42]

you will be 'forever young'
stupid old cunt

jim ferguson

own every word
in every language

own every one
own every thing

and die so peacefully
in your sleep

so peaceful in

achieving a feeling of peace
all because

you've taken back control—
pity you let it get so far away

in the first place
teenage women

in the Western World
have bigger breasts now

this question is important
the clothes maketh the (wo)man

the bra maketh the woman
all your identities wrapped

in foil, eternally fresh
eternal as your youth

the ocean is a frightening place to drown!
Elixir, Ambrosia, Honey in the pots

dripping with golden sun
photosynthesis   energy

jim ferguson

random quanta
pick one peculiar planet

make it conscious
and call your *self* god

The Sun God
make it simple

it is
and it is not

from a distance it all looks calm
but when you're in amongst it

torrid, totally raging, insane
burn you, fry you

shrivel and spit you
roasted

utterly done
totally undone

unravelled, finished
fucked and gone

take back control
steak-bake control

if there's one word you want to control
it is *cunt*

that or *revolution*

very rubbery
fake feta cheese

jim ferguson

wont help you
bounce back home

drunk woman
drunk man

walking that way
you want the cars

to kill you
knock you out cold

quick
and
gone

just was
just is

just ice

call it justice

(just-)

no profit in prophets
if you don't catch them young,
wring everything out
of labour that they've done,

when they are empty
make a feast of their bones,
there's another generation
and another generation
you can load-up
your greed-system on

jim ferguson

sell them short-skirts and wide-hats
sell them the whole lot
of every...
of all the everythings they made

and all you did was wash your face
in ice-cold water filled with rats,
you were busy making laws
as that old saying goes

no laws for the rich
while the poor rot in your jails,
that's what you call it
on and on

(-ice)

is your enemy my enemy
is your enemy my friend?

call it justice
see how they dance

from zero to England in one easy step
havent you had enough yet?

on March 30th 1798 martial law was
declared
across Ireland

Tom Moore,43 in nom de plume,
called upon his countryfolk to rise

for sad was the state of Ireland
under the Brits

and strange that in

jim ferguson

April 1807

cobbler John Struthers
was on his way to visit Tannahill in Paisley

the same Tannahill who esteemed Tom Moore
'the Anacreon of the age'

and in this year of 2020
the Govt are crying out

for youths to join police Force
for sure when all the unemployed

are counted, the police
will have a job on their hands

to simply keep them calm!
Not since the 1980s

have we seen unemployment
rise so steeply

ThATCHER's ghost returning,
Damn! that's fuckin creepy

worse than fuckin creepy,
Brit imperial history

is less than filled with glory
from James Cook[44] in Hawaii

to Windrush[45]
and the NHS betrayed

difficult to know
if those British Tories

are merely
bumbling fools of idiocy

or carleess bastards
who's only plan

is to steal our public money
and lock it in some secret bank off-shore

—see how they dance!

"... it is odd to see how stories fly— You
recollect the song- "When time who steals
our Years away." It is not Thos Campbell's
as was supposed- it is written by a Thomas
Moore, whom I esteem as the Anacreon of the
age I have seen a volume of his in which was
the song alluded to - like old Dibdin he
usually composes Music to his own words -
the Edin[b] reviewers have endeavour'd to cut
him up for being too loose in his subjects
- I will write you one Epigram

Your Mother says, my little venus!
There's something not correct between us,
   And you're in fault as much as I;
Now, on my soul, my little venus!
I think 'twould not be right between us
   To let your mother tell a lie ....[46]

----

may day moon
hangs in the sky

jim ferguson

delicious shades
of blue and gray

blurred clouds
and crystal clear light

like
the end of days

in the afternoon
looking out

the window
watching the moon

————————

you want
to talk about

your
creative process

as if you're
the only person

who has such a thing

who has such a thing?
lots of people

rely on accident
accident to find
the creative spark
a thought
that accidently

lands in your
head

Yes that's it
i get you

like accidental prose
falling from the

S k y

You		we	i		they
are		are	am		are

sitting home watching The Dickensian news
cold-hearted capital was doing little good
digging deeper in to its philanthropic core
left my human heart bruised and sore
nothing much improved since 1964
even with technology that gleams

Accidental Prose – 19 Short News Stories

You wonder what to do with a house full of silence. Sell it. Silence is a highly marketable commodity these days. Think of the all mega-cities, in any one of those cities you could sell houses full of silence for an absolute fortune. It's a bad joke and accidental but in this case silence really is golden.
*

Hail! Toilers at the coalface of miserable existence:

jim ferguson

consider the frequent floods that blight your lives; the torrents of dead birds that fall from the sky and fierce winds that crush and flatten everything in their path. They are no accident. Look to your vehicles, if you have such, and to decade upon decade of burning fossil fuels. Then curse those who doubted global warming. Especially the bearded phoney ecologist who sought sanctuary in the antipodes after, it's alleged, taking dubious money from oil interests.

*

I told you he was dead grumpy the last time I met him. This was before his stroke. I should've seen it coming because he was very unlike himself but everything is easy with hindsight. He calls it his accident. He's euphemistic, and philosophical, glad to be alive you might say.

*

Martin Eden, accidently on purpose, fell out of a port-hole. It was like he was the Master Ludi from the *Glass Bead Game*. I've never come across two novels with such similar endings. Both books appear to suggest that there is something about drowning that is somehow redemptive. What percentage of suicides has been by drowning? What percentage has been accidental and not suicide at all? If you try to think of all the recorded suicides in the history of humanity, factor in the inevitability of human error, it is only rational to conclude that some of those 'recorded suicides' must be errors. Accidents, no less than just a poor soul who has gone for a swim in some river or sea and been drowned by circumstances outwith their control; the attribution of suicide coming from a certain weight of evidence that those who remain alive were wont to sift. The problem is of course the dead won't tell us. The poet Robert Tannahill of Paisley is a particularly poignant

jim ferguson

case in this regard. Was his drowning in the night of May 17 1810 an accident? Was it a warm night in May and he was merely trying to cool down? Or was it a deliberate act? The evidence points to suicide but in truth we really can't be sure. There is room for doubt, and there is room to doubt doubt also, a fascinating problem for someone like David Hume to consider. Alas Hume had died in 1776 at which time Tannahill was but two years of age and without a poem or song to his name. And Hume on his death bed perhaps not realising quite the gravity with which history twists us round its grubby little fingers, or perhaps, all too aware of the accidental nature of time.

*

It was only a persona of you. You and not you: a dangerously dark sycophantic ranter; an accidental antichrist.

*

Only the police understand what motivates murderers...

...them, and somehow by accident, Agatha Christie.

*

You encourage decay. You are walking entropy, a dead energy without the necessary zeal to forestall the chaos you create and attract. You fall into it. You're a living accident. Things plummet and break. Living things die, and somehow it all comes down to the second law of thermodynamics. Apparently "entropy wins when organisms cease to take in energy and die." Shit, eh?

jim ferguson

*

Speaking personally... Is there any other way to speak? Maybe ventriloquism but that apart of course I am speaking for myself. What I really mean is, intimately speaking: to communicate with you now on intimate terms I'll share a thought I do not usually express out loud; *how disgusting I find it to have been born in the same country as the poet Robert Burns*. This is in fact only an accident of birth, but let's face it birth is the biggest accident that happens in life. The only people you can blame for this monstrous mishap are your poor unsuspecting parents. The fools, why didn't they take precautions?

Anyway, to return to Robert Burns, (whose dates are 1659 to 1796): so it was in 1659 when the first accident occurred in the life of Burns and sometime in the January of that year he was, indeed, quite accidently, born. I need only hear a few syllables of the man's poetry to be instantly filled with a total hatred for all things Scottish, including myself. Were Burns to have never existed perhaps I would have been spared the torture of such self-loathing. What's worse is that my memory now fails me and I can't really remember which came first. Was I really driven to self loathing by the poetry of Robert Burns. Or did I already loath myself and only realise it fully when I heard the poems of Burns in Primary 2. Ah childhood, that's a river I'll never be diving into again.

Another thing about Burns is that he appears to have had an incredible longevity, apparently only dying eventually at the age of one hundred and thirty six or seven. Nice work if you can get it.
*

This is certainly **not** poetry.

Nor is it a saucepan. It's not even a pipe. Even in

jim ferguson

French, *Ceci n'est pas une pipe.* Mmmmm ... *n'est pas une pipe ... pipe.*

I know you stole that, Rene Magritte, you can't fool me; an accident my arse.

*

Try not to be pre-occupied with other moments, try to live in the moment you're in... You're like a Buddhist when you're at the hairdressers, in the haircutting moment ... in my experience, and yes ... I think your haircut turned out quite well. I'm very bad at the small conversations with the hair-cutting people. If you are too perhaps we should stay at home together and cut each others' hair. You think so? No, too risky. I'd never accidentally cut off your ear. That's crazy. A modern Van Gough, no chance, I can't even paint a wall.

This is not a painting of a wall.

*

How she forgets things these days. She's forgotten herself and other people. Everyone knows the terrifying sadness of it. There but for the grace of god and all that nonsense. It has a pathology like any other illness. It's not an accident of life, it is not inevitable. There are treatments, there will be better treatments. Our understanding remains at a fairly early stage but medical interventions are possible. We are all doomed to die but not to lose ourselves while still rich in life. Let optimism flourish. Let Glasgow flourish; birds, bells, trees and fishes.

*

jim ferguson

For excellence in the specific field of creating an internet connection through a large fruit-cake or pudding (what the Scots call a cloughty-dumpling) and showing how the network connection may be enhanced by the use of additional custard she was awarded the Andrew Carnegie Memorial Award. The award reflects the recipient's truly revolutionary contribution to technological advancement in the 21st century.

Later, the addition of the custard was discovered to have been a laboratory accident during the lunch hour. This woman was no Marie Curie and didn't like anything radioactive. Never the less because of the erudition of her paper on the subject the award was allowed to stand.

*

I told the publisher that there was no prospect of my writing a biography of the invisible woman. She hadn't left a trace of her existence anywhere. I told them I couldn't write about a woman who had so totally expunged herself from all and any possible historical narratives. It would be like trying to draw a blank, a character without definition. H. G. Wells managed to write the story of the invisible man back in 1897 but his invisible man had accidently left a trail behind. In reality, or at a subconscious level, Wells's man did not want to be invisible. But this woman, she really knew what she was doing. She was a fantastic success and by dint of her triumph her story must remain untold, at least by me. She was and remains the historical equivalent of what physicists call 'dark matter'.

*

The narrators were accidently omnipotent. However, the entire book was apocryphal. God it makes you wonder if anything's true. Loaves and fishes... an accident... surely not?

*

Even if *The Bucket Rider* was already dead it is clear that Kafka was very familiar with the concept of fuel-poverty. This thoroughly vindicates my view that the arrest of Josef K was no accident. K's arrest was in fact the expression of an ideological terror campaign akin to the deliberate denial of access to food, medicine, water and fuel that a large minority of the world's population experience today. Where was K's access to justice? Where is any one's? How the impoverished freeze in winter: it is heart warming that a cursory study of literature enlightens us so: though art can't stop them from freezing anymore than religion can.

*

I was very gently trying to squeeze the puss from a spot on the forehead of a friend when accidently and without warning the damn thing exploded, filling my eyes with custardy goo. 'God that was sore,' said my friend. 'I'm blind, I'm blind,' I replied.

*

You miserable starvelings who blight the lives of the cheerfully wealthy! Return to your bombed out villages, crumbling dwellings and relatives who are too sick to travel, there's nothing for you here. But should you accidently choose to stay, we can accidently bomb your villages again and again and again.

*

The problem with art is that people, who ever *people* are, expect some kind of shape and form. Whoever *they* are, they expect a beginning, a middle and an end, or a dénouement. Or, something they can interpret as having a certain and definite meaning. Mostly this is a mistake, an accident. Life is not like that, mostly, and neither is art. Music has the greatest freedom but even in music I feel a certain circumscription. Circumscription! Not the easiest word to say. It contains its own meaning. The pronunciation of circumscription is circumscribed. I could go on.

No.
I won't.

*

Here comes Jesus. He was accidently betrayed by Judas you know.
Merry Christmas!

ding dong ☺

part 3. There is Music in Romanticism

There is music in Romanticism (you know)

Rogers & Campbell,
Moore & Byron
all were friendly Whigs
entwined within The Romantic

they loved to Satirise The Tories
but were not themselves devoid of pompous hours
amongst the claret and lobster courses
rounded off with Brandy!

Coarse! apparently they were not,
yet each in his own way mis-fitted
early nineteenth-century life,
Napoleonic strife and the like

though never too dishonourable
to dine out with their pistols exposed
cock-sure, hair-triggered, duellists
and I suppose hereto (here too) one must

make mention of Francis Jeffrey[47]
so to not be ill-mannered and grey
by omission of certain facts
pertaining to *The Scandal*

of the Missing Bullets... Of which
The Prince Regent made little
though sent Lord Moira off to India
for all his trifling trouble. Of course

The Regent being much distracted
by the madness of his father

jim ferguson

was often busy taking succour
from the ample breasts of Protestant
extremists

Who ever heard of such? Religious
extremism
in the bosom of England, surely never?
In that green and pleasant land
of all that's fair and tolerant.

> Alas,
> but yes.
> Yes, yes, yes
> so riddled with religious passion and avarice

> Fair England furnished Moore et al
> with copious bullets and excess powder
> with which, in wild abandon,
> they let their satires fly with due aplomb and
> style

> Alas,
> but yes.
> Oh yes   yes   yes

> Aw fuck aye
> twas ever thus
> alas

> *yur jokin! naw!*
> *naw-naw naw, naw-naw, naw-naw*

> oh but aye
> ya tadger

> the long-nosed plague has come

to snuff us out

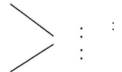

ant-eater, yummmmmmmmm

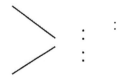

you just don't care

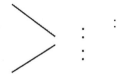

with your nonchalant tea-cake addiction

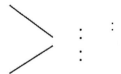

crisps and chocolate, ya fucker

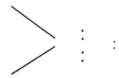

antibiotics, anti-depressants and pain-killers

jim ferguson

too

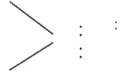

diabetes and heart disease

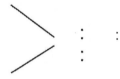

mental instability

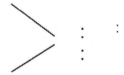

i'm fully in charge of my mental health

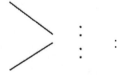

an abundance of human brain cells

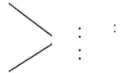

tea and toast and a toffee crisp

jim ferguson

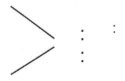

and crisps: a toffee crisp and crisps and nuts,
dry-roasted

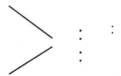

strapped to a large settee

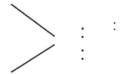

watching endless streams on Netflix

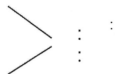

wearing a nappy

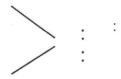

or stay dry panty-liners that absorb all odours

jim ferguson

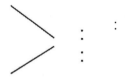

we're doing a survey

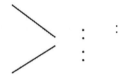

how many mouse-clicks or screen taps
do you use on average
when making a purchase?

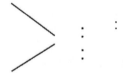

too many?
more than one is too much money

the ideal would be?

NONE!

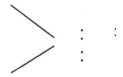

nothing is too much for you

jim ferguson

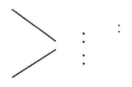

absolute zero
remains our unattainable goal

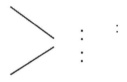

anything is too much for you

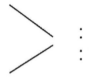

attainable or not we'll seize it
absolute zero
absolute cold

the irony is
our means of seizure will be
accidental global warming

:

:

jim ferguson

we don't care about Kafka
or his 'Bucket Rider'
or his cold
or his TB death
or his corpse beneath
that bloody white sheet
crimson stained
with blood from his
oversensitive
Bohemian lungs
Franz can fuck off
fuck off Franz
get to fuck out
out of our Protestant only heaven

heaven not for Catholics
heaven not for Jews
heaven not for Shiites
heaven not for Sunniites
heaven not for Anarchiites
heaven not for Hindiioos

heaven for Protestants only

fuck off with your Catholic Emancipations
with your Irish Nationalisms
with your Scottish Independencies

with your Greek and your Italian and your Pole
and your boney French and your wild gaulle
fuck off everyone and all!
no welcome here, here it's

heaven for White English Gentlemen Protestants
only

this is not for everybody
how strange that it should be
'Anarchist Entertainment
Not for Everybody'[48]
for the mere deserving few

know not what they do!
heaven for Protestants only

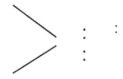

Satirising the super rich

1. gets you nowhere
2. gets you dead
3. gets you a holiday in the Bahamas
4. none of the above

we're doing a survey
designed by Saint Peter

We know from Scripture that heaven is a real place.
Please read all terms and conditions carefully to avoid
disappointment.

jim ferguson

"And I tell you Peter, and on this rock I will build my church and the gates of hell shall not prevail against it. I will give you the keys of the Kingdom of Heaven, and whatever you bind on earth shall be bound in heaven, and whatever you loose on earth shall be loosed in heaven."[49]

Disappointment makes its inevitable appearance. Ineluctably, one may add.

Fuck off, Franz!
You're way too gloomy, ya bastard.

who on earth
could ever perform
such a dance as this?

other than
Graham Fulton's
'19th Century Romantic poet with

consumption
made of icing sugar'[50]

someone aught to bring out a book:
"Kafka and the Romantics:
a study of fleeting footsteps"
see it! — how it runs up and down

the lists
of best sellers
books of the year

prizewinning favourites
of stars and
celebrities

who's little lives
are just as fleeting
as anybody elses'

poor deluded bastards
who imagine themselves
angels

ascending
into their
white and protestant heaven

because they are
special

because they are
exceptional

and yet

all of us are

jim ferguson

special

we are all
exceptional

in that simple sense
of being

about the same as
everyone else:

who on earth
could ever perform
such a blinding dance as this?

my sun
          your sun
                    sun in the sky

simple and bewildering

shines just a little longer
than your
average human
                    lifespan

and that old bastard
Henry Ford
wondered how it was done

and still poor Kafka,
old or young,
died of consumption

while still on trial
for being
who

on earth
could perform
such a dance
      as this

————

someone seeking
dignity

with a voice
like

Billie Holiday

some one
seeking

dignity
with Albert Camus'
clarity[51]

————

Camus
saw so clearly

the beauty
of setting

the executioners
free

from their onerous
task

of political

jim ferguson

state-sanctioned

murder

and yet
where once

piety held
the political hands

science now
takes that grip

while truth from lies
remains, as ever,

as difficult to decipher:
s/he who pays the piper

and money's-worth
not human-worth

still rules
— or thrashes so relentlessly to do —

wouldst that
Shelley[52]
and
Moore
and Paisley Boy
Tannahill
had been right
that we'd
'no cast out and fecht like brutes'[53]
but settle all political disputes
with poems
and tunes

jim ferguson

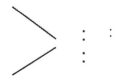

There is music in Romanticism (you know)

such is the drift for dignity
so many years since

Frrrrrrrrrrrrrrrrrrrrrrrrrrrrrrrrrrrrrrrrrrrr
France
endeavoured
ttttttttttttttttttttttto
set the civilised

world free

with maverick
Bonaparte
waging
global war

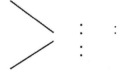

There is music in Romanticism (you know)

jim ferguson

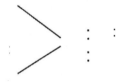

avoiding suicide her/his only ambition

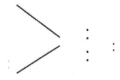

wary of the wonder of ideals are we

perhaps and maybe not

who wants to look at the same fucking font
all day?

i baptise thee Fire
i baptise thee Light of the Sun
i baptise thee Free of Ambition and Charity
i baptise thee Graceful

i baptise thee fuck all
such ritual is not necessary
dignity will simply sing
in your dance and free-style song

grandiose ritual is exactly where

jim ferguson

Bonaparte went wrong

let all authority crumble
*who wants to look at the same fucking font
all day?*

*perhaps the whale and dolphin
are beyond us already*
human fools that we are

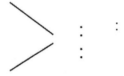

such a handy blend of
philanthropy
and
misanthropy

can't stop the entropy increasing

time only moves in one direction
as we -as we- can see that's predetermined

even if
nothing else

is

this is an elegant bull-dozer

jim ferguson

bullshit
this is a turd born cold

worn old
and ready

for death.
goddard

goddard
what happened to my thesis on Goddard

goddard

edited it out

owing to a lack
of any understanding

of his oeuvre
this all too Beckettian

Viconian and Lacanian[54]

Yir fuckin arse!

this is the kind of thing
that brings the academy into disrepute

it will surely mean expulsion

expulsion from the university
and beyond!

but i don't ... to be outside the universe

it is your job to be curious

it is your job to explore

extemporise, crucial that you look beyond
crumbling empires wasting away

everything has to die someday!
being a gloom merchant   beyond

is your forte
alas please please please

don't maim the beautiful
with the ugly

it all has to be in there
ugly, beautiful, nondescript

it's a handbook on how
to make the non-poetic

poetic, some think
it started with Wordsworth

and Coleridge
those lyrical balladeers

but the Greeks
had gone there

centuries before
everything

was unfounded and
unbound

endless energetic tap-dancing
wears out your mind

jim ferguson

as well as your shoes

who on earth
could ever perform
such anarchic dancing as this?

jim ferguson

part 4. As Freely as you Love

bonjour ...yet another
oven-ready
aesthetic theory
of sugary beauty

is so unnecessary

catch that rabbit
silly boy blue[55]

no one is left
to help you   *here*

*the original damage
was done*

all those right-wing
girls and boys

privately immersed
in private joy

oblivious to the hurt and carnage
they cause others and the planet

*sorry, sorry, sorry,
they can't help it*

*the boarding schools
they were all brought up in*

is the origin of the damage   *done
like*

                                        jim ferguson

an original
sin

yes,
all those bullet-faced
Bankers and Chancers

If I was impolite
I'd call them thankless

but on second thought
they really are wankers

toot toot toot, Betty Boop!

they know they're outnumbered
but always push democracy down

by means of finance and law,
hectoring police,

cultural, physical mercenaries
always mopping up history

until the multitude get angry
and cannot be controlled anymore

cannot be controlled any longer
and you'll see those tired old statues tumble

if the multitude are wise:
I'd say they're wiser now

it is not 1789 anymore

yet another
oven-ready

jim ferguson

aesthetic theory
of sugary beauty

and financial rules
and social regulations
will give way
to robust and plural democracy —

an aesthetics of everything
from deepest gloom
to piercing light
from the ugly to the sublime

is
so
necessary

Is that fuckin right?
I doubt it.

who on earth?
Okay, I'm sorry to say the state of
your body has come as quite a shock.
The aging process has ravaged you.
Being a vain fuckwit it has made
you quite depressed: you have the
devastated body of 60 year old
male who has lived neither well nor
wisely. Your mind remains around
the age 45, a psychological lag of
some significance. You say the last 15
years, from 45 to 60 have been very
long and that you hope your mind
catches up with your body soon, all
because you don't want to die at the

jim ferguson

somewhat youthful mental age of 52 or 53. Such a waste of thoughtful capacity, your fully functioning mind consigned to the grave through the action of your merciless and ravaged physical state. Your powers of diagnosis appear accurate and realistic. You'd have thought that evolution would have come up with some sort of solution to your problem. Evolution, alas, is a haughty and independent cat. It cares not a fuck for the thoughts of humanity — even if those thoughts are part of evolution itself, evolution is blissfully lacking in self-awareness. Beyond any immediate vacuum, such a science has no interest in the ego-driven psychological minor ailments of one human individual. Which is, evidently, all that you are. Okay...

N E X T – *next*[56]

work to live becomes its opposite

Il travaille plus que moi.
Elle travaille plus que moi.
Il travaille pour le gouvernement.

Elle travaille pour le gouvernement.
Il travaille plus.
Elle travaille plus.

I don't know where you left your jacket

under the rock
where the spiders thrive

it's ruined now
totally useless

if it gets too cold
I'll freeze to death

dance the dance
of death to warm your heart

gloomy bastard
surely we can all have a decent

jacket from all the beautiful bounty
our sweet blue planet Earth

has to offer nothing
you can take for granted

money doesn't grow on trees
yes it does, money grows inside

everything the earth creates
I suppose, all you have to do

is warm it, *that's it, yes,*
Prometheus unbound[57]

a bold usurper,
the very point

where humanity found
its feet

Is that fuckin right?

jim ferguson

I doubt it.

———

work to live becomes its opposite
see how we've robbed this fuckin planet
ha ha : ha ha : haaaaaaaaaaaaaaaaaaa

and

If Donnie Trump could sing like Colonel
Mustard[58]
Perhaps he would not be a horrid bastard

Is that fuckin right?
I doubt it.
ha ha : ha ha : haaaaaaaaaaaaaaaaaaa

barely into long trousers
Donnie ran
a multi-national

corporation
from the back left corner
of his Y-fronts drawer

he soon expanded
to the right

the line carries the language
and
the language carries the line
language takes the weight,
it does the heavy lifting
all you have to do is warm it up
— nature gives it to you

a gift from the Earth

often difficult to destroy
but always possible too
witness the nuclear,
fission and fusion,

incredibly difficult for us to do
nature does not hand it to us
as easily as it gives us language
dancing through air and across the page
travaille terminé

Il travaille pour le gouvernement.

Elle travaille pour le gouvernement.

who among us knows what love is?

dynamo wheels
turning and churning
weaving an infinite pattern
of ruined hope

comes home
with petrol-station-flowers
outstretched before sarcastic eyes
— see how they roll —

who would try a smile
at mindless symbols
sent from Cupid's
corpulent arms
— all marketing charm —

love is an old concussed heart

jim ferguson

love is a tired still-true heart
love is sentimental education
love waits for years at stations

always
hopeful

always
deceitful

always true
on target, comes the piercing dart,

love is elation that harms you
love makes you blue
love is a rainbow
love kisses, kicks and tortures you

love makes you
                   — a rainbow too —

Q. What makes the following equivalents?

a) run a mile
b) jump a stile
c) eat a country-pancake

Write an essay that proves you know
what love is. Illustrate your essay with at
least two examples of equivalence from
a), b) or c) above.

empty hearts make the most noise

it isn't hearts it's heads

that's right, yes
that's what they said

at the last meeting of the
Society for the Suppression of Vice[59]

in 1885,
which was very-very very-very nice!

yes, those moralists destroyed
and blighted many many lives

of women and the urban poor
who could not abjure

the urge to procreate
outwith wedlock

or even at length profess
an atheistic bent

indeed,
no pun intended,

but men were always men
and ever put their cocks in

women, ah how we long for such
these days
as that wondrous
Society for the Suppression of Vice

when we need a place for everyone

jim ferguson

and
everyone in their place

Is that fuckin right?
I doubt it.

Do you think they knew about love?

as our good friend Joseph Roth[60] proclaimed:
all good women would rather love a bullfighter
than bother with the ballot box,
in prose that brimmed with types
including the perfectly ripe
and troubling metaphorical nose

ah, holy drinker, such a notion
would not wash its face
these days, post-holocaust, of course,
of course

the world is now a different place
where swastika painted men defend
Winston Churchill's right to racism
poor England lies confused amidst
shreds of bleating anachronism

those Scotobrits aye were sleekit
marching shoulder to shoulder
round the world with old John Bull
enslaving all before them in the name of progress
and left poor Erin starving in her bed

the shame of it, the shame
must be repaired, if we're brave enough
at last, to stand ourselves,
and if not, ever to remain
a nation of guilt, deceit, humiliation   *shame*

Do you think they know what love is?

bring all
the yelling fighters home
to sing a song of peace,
of freedom and of plenty

alas
there's still   a price to pay
for
the   success of idiots
throughout history

wheel out your favourite anti-humans
and slice the heids ayont the shoodirs
be just like them, and just as foolish
gaze open-mouthed upon the restoration

of the Bourbons, *this isn't 1814 again*
we know what love is now, don't we?

we do not cure such running sores with leeches,
no panic in our sleekit, timorous, breeches
these allegoricals will not hold together,
your history flows all wrong like some weird river

Is that fuckin right?
I doubt it.

———————

certain ideas
relate

the nation
state

jim ferguson

to nothing
more than

a mental illness

————————

the intimacy
of Sartre and de Beauvoir

mandarins with souls of iron,
and generous hearts

or Arendt[61] puzzling
the nature of evil

— banal bureaucracy
from which no one dissents

at least no one important
in the market place of ideas

all of which sounds just the way
global capitalism is today

who would have thought it,
what degrees of freedom shall we tolerate

we give the system of capital
total control and the planet warms up

trees fall and roll, mass extinctions
they say they follow
the rule of law
but we know the capitalists

are the biggest gangsters
everywhere you look

there's private security
and dubious what

the role of the police is—
and if you want to apportion blame

blame it all on Plato
to start with

no one had to believe
a word Plato said

perhaps Hitler understood that
innately, in his confluence of history,

it took the red army
to send adolf off to bed

others helped
and had their grief

in brothels run by
Hermann Goering

history is a shocking place to live
something to be thought about

but mustn't stop
creation of the new
when we give the police consent
we must retain right of dissent
first and foremost amongst
all qualities of public debate *-dissent*

jim ferguson

—ach fur fuck's sake
geeza brrek

I draw the line at fascism
aye good, cause if you let them in

they would not let you live
n aw the hate that lives within

authoritarian minds combined
would never let you love

as freely as you love
the beautiful now

the future dead, the past
a synthesis of slaves and cruelty

everyone ruled by brutes
and brutish systematic laws

that lie beyond dissension
— if you want to know where you go

when you die
try dissenting now —

capitalism never sleeps
the rich remain

its hyperactive servile
hoarders, piling money

without knowing the meaning
or simplicity of enough

— stand still and you die

jim ferguson

keep moving and you die

remove your gloomy shoes
and shine them up

with spit and polish
recall the joyous moment of your birth

the joyous shock of creation
'prometheus unbound'

absolute potential for boundless laughter
on stage the comedies rage

and Brecht
puffs his old cigar

how far can we go
humanity

vaulting higher still — *for all*
batman is a riddler at heart

don't travel there
if you want an allegorical

superhero at least
have the decency to invent your own

fucked-up dystopian vision
sing that beautiful song
'feels like prison
lah-lah lah-lah'

i'm not a machine
although i know

jim ferguson

algorithms are busy
interpreting my data

as if it were my soul

fancy that? not much, not really

i doubt the efficacy
of any anti-viral vaccine

the digital machine
the capitalist machine
the political machine
the kultural machine
all melting

into one dimension
what now for knowing (?)

consciousness

or future plans
relent with the relentlessness

take a rest

learn of love in labour
of natural work in labour
determine your own story

by whose hands
does the future
come to pass

the moment
of your birth
brought us so much

jim ferguson

we never could
have imagined
without your

all encompassing
aesthetic
the ultimate in ugly

not plural
being as
we forgot

what made us beautiful

irony the only defence
against becoming
an evil parody

of what all our potential
and future selfish selfs
might be love

of nothing more than
mere consumption
do not let the fear

grip us, alone,
amidst decay
unloved,
you are not meant to read it that way
you are not meant to write it that way
say something, love, dont drown

be courageous in small gestures
do enough to keep swimming
beautifully in the morning light

jim ferguson

your satire shines as beacon of hope
yir lanwij izza wunnir
no boredom in thi middla Europe

hark et something awthigether new
oan ivri angle human
no thi fuckwit cock of empire

no pain
no domination
simple pleasure

sharin
luv jist screivin
oor ain story

in that wee boat
the ship of dignity
ithir than slavery

happily watery
swimming inside
an aye universal

placenta
of somethin
luvvin

aw the time
n
jist furra minute

aye
aye aye
aw fuck aye

jim ferguson

uv course
sweet smiler
plural and priceless

jazz in a church of equality
singin yir ain stories
painliss, diffrint, happy

in oor disagreements
renouncin aw authority
but that tae be thi authors

uv oor ain stories
free n flyin
in a bright

conception
uv luv
hand n hand

wae honesty
we will defy
thon bitter agony

forget oor selfish selfs
in the process
of becoming *we* ... oui, aye,

affirmative
uv aw   (of all)

nae race
nae class
nae gender
humanity, at last ...

_____

jim ferguson

we don't live here
as individuals
or en masse
unaware of our own mortality

and that of others
-something martial
in our nature
hunter and the hunted

predator and prey
big cats come
take you away
you're merely a label to them

a satiation
and a food source

Okay, so he was lying in bed early one
morning when they arrived in his flat.
He was a young man. His mother had
not been dead very long. It would not
be an exaggeration to say that the grief

was killing him. Or the alcohol. He was drinking more than too much more than most days. He lived alone, simply but comfortably. Quite warm and cosy. He had good plumbing and clean running water: electricity: books and art on his walls: music, tv and a digital connection. It couldn't be called absolute poverty. He was clean and somewhat fastidious. He smoked both tobacco and marijuana but rarely took any medicines from the human pharmacopeia of painkilling and mind-numbing pills. He had an idea that most of the modern synthetic drugs were to a large extent untested. Alcohol and hashish were ancient drugs. Their usage stretched back millennia. Valium he figured was only just over half of one century old. He knew people that had been around longer. So if you were going to put any kind of poisonous or mind-altering substances into your body it was probably best to stick with those which were naturally occurring or had been in use for more than a thousand years. Tobacco of course was a waste of time and money, yet of all things, this was his most serious and harmful addiction. Not only was tobacco slowly killing him but it had been a mainstay of the economics of the slave-trade: that itself should have been ample reason for him to quit smoking. Alas addiction outweighed principle. He needed tobacco as much as he needed electricity. Without the latter none of his devices of modern life would function; his connection to wider society would crumble. He was in bed, nursing both grief and

jim ferguson

hangover, when they arrived to disconnect
the electricity. At first he'd heard vague
sounds in the distance, he thought he was
dreaming, his muscles aching and dull, his
mouth rather dry, skin dampish, a mixture
of clingy and sweaty. He put a pillow
over his head the better to sleep it all off.
He felt the hand of Morpheus upon his
shoulder only it wasn't Morpheus at all it
was a Sheriff's Officer. He sat up startled.
Was this a flat invasion? 'Who the fuck are
you?'
'Wake up, we're here to disconnect you?'
The officer handed him an envelope and
left him without closing his bedroom door.
He could hear mens' voices talking and
laughing, and the hammering started
almost immediately. He got out of bed.
Dressed and opened the envelope. He
had not paid his electricity bill since
his mother had died. There was now a
locksmith to pay for and additional costs
which amounted to as much as the actual
electricity he'd used but not yet paid for.
He felt somewhat like Josef K must have
done when 'he knew he had done nothing
wrong but, one morning, he was arrested'.
 Capitalism was predator, our young man
prey, and The Law the stage-scenery upon
which our play was acted out. Okay,

———————

how could he be so naive
it's anybody's guess

thing is
he'd always paid his bills before

so was unaware
of how the system attacks

ignorance is no excuse
and hiding inside one's own grief

is an unhealthy place to be
even although

through it all
he managed

to keep his job
at least

that was something
yes, but he hated his job

it was useless
mindless work

washing the dishes of the wealthy
fucksake

of course, which ever way
he turned, all encompassing

capitalism had him cornered
only a slither of liberal democracy

made it almost bearable
otherwise to endure

you'd have to revert to animal

jim ferguson

and instincts of survival

where would morality
wander then?

right out the fucking window
is what I'd contend

agreed?
   agreed

kafka understood
he worked in insurance!

————

————

 we may have previous wisdoms
humanity yet contained

in the ancient poetry
of wandering chinese

rebels

surely nothing better than
a gun boat!

————

————

body image is everything

toppled from the forest
of your deep affections
all gone wrong

how cold the ground
you lie in
                    where never a soul is smiling
the rhythm ends
                    dear departed
sweetest rhythm stilled now

                    looks are not an issue
anymore

_____
_____

ask not what Betty Blue[62]
            can do for you
but what you can do
            for Betty Blue

Le petit déjeuner est prêt mon amour
Sortez vos casseroles et poêles

from tethered sleep
poison begets poison
the romantics among us
must proceed with caution

red sheet, body afloat
alive with rolled cigarette

breathing, sunlight,
aloof clouds

Up
—which of these are suitable as the title for
your painting?—
open curtains
open windows

jim ferguson

micro-waved porridge
banana
pealed banana
milk in porcelain bowl (white)
a comment on the world wide web
wooden floor (man varnishing)
on-line chores
on-line chit chat
a new front door
a dead body (13 months old)
workmen
glaswegians
glaswegian dogs
man on stairs
woman in park
photographers
ducks
duck pond
poet reading zadie smith
sunset
crows
study of a beetle
smiling corpse
night sky with porridge

————
————

from tethered sleep
passion begets passion
the romantics among us
must proceed with caution

the mattress arrived
on 7th March 2018

though new and red
not very comfortable

but made my dreams more sexual
—is that something you really want to share?

it's fiction

it is fiction, and beyond
some commentary on political philosophy
I really think we're done here
are we done

yes, aye,
i think we're done here

agreed,
           agreed

always always, never never

you bare the loss
            the absent heart
you're trying to lose weight
            or not get too fat
you look like a dancing kitty-cat

meow meow

moments gone

jim ferguson

Notes

1. On February 5th 2004 23 undocumented migrant workers were drowned in Morecambe Bay, Lancashire. It was reported that they worked in conditions of modern slavery as cockle pickers.
2. Charles Darwin (1809-1882), naturalist and author of 'On the Origin of Species' first published 1859.
3. Donald John Trump (b.1946), far-right and highly divisive 45th President of the Republic of the United States of America.
4. George Robertson (b.1946), Sometime Scottish Labour MP, Privy Councillor and Defence Minister in the Blair government. He was Secretary General of NATO: The North Atlantic Treaty Organisation (1999-2004). He took a seat in the British House of Lords as Baron Robertson of Port Ellen in 1999.
5. A paraphrase of Samuel Beckett (1906-1989), 'Imagination Dead Imagine' first published in French in 1965. Irish novelist, dramatist and Nobel prize winner.
6. Galileo Galilei (1564-1642) Italian astronomer, mathematician and engineer who came into conflict with the Catholic Church over his heliocentric views. He is the subject of Brecht's play 'The Life of Galileo': 1st version written in 1938, a play much concerned with the problems of resistance to both brute-authority and unyielding-ideology.
7. Michel Nostradamus (1503-1566), French mystic, physician, occultist and author of 'The Prophecies' (1555), consisting of 942 quatrains.
8. Swiss Cheese, one of the sons of Mother Courage in Brecht's play 'Mother Courage and her Children' translated into Scots by Tom Leonard (Smokestack Books, Middleborough, 2014). Bertold Brecht (1898-1956), German poet and playwright.
9. See the movie 'Taxi Driver' (1976). Directed by Martin Scorsesi.
10. Rainer Maria Rilke (1875-1926), Bohemian poet and writer.
11. IED: Improvised Explosive Device.
12. Guido Fawkes, aka Guy Fawkes, was a member of a group who planned the failed Gunpowder Plot of 1605. Lately the name adopted by a far right political blogger: "Guido Fawkes is a right-wing website published by British-Irish political blogger Paul Staines," (Wikipedia, July 2020).
13. Paraphrase of Scottish rock singer Alex Harvey (1935-1982): "considered the situation", in the song 'The Man in the Jar'.
14. René Daumal (1908-1944), French para-surrealist poet, prose writer and practitioner of pataphysics.

15. Robert McLean (1961-2017), Paisley born musician (bass player, pianist, guitarist and drummer).

16. This line points to the connection between René Daumal's 'A Night of Serious Drinking' and the ideas of George Ivanovich Gurdjieff (1877?-1949): the latter was an Armenian salesman, composer, mystic and guru concerned with spiritual and mental wellbeing through 'The Work of the 4th Way'; which may or not have a whiff of chancerism but certainly isn't dull. The Fourth Way involves attaining a heightened apprehension of reality through exercises in introspection and reduction of ego. What Rilke was getting at in his 'Angel' poems, Daumal in 'Le Contra Ciel' and the teachings of Gurdjieff, appeared to me to have certain points of intersection or overlap concerning the realisation of self knowledge leading to familiarity with the concept that human beings are not the centre of the universe which ultimately leads to reduced anxiety. If you get my drift?

17. Franz Kafka (1883-1924), Bohemian novelist and short story writer.

18. NOMENCLATURA: A means of assigning names: One who holds authority by permission of a higher authority: The process of assigning authority: Holder of high office particularly in the Soviet Union.

19. Tom Leonard, 'being a human being: for Mordechai Vanunu'.

20. Refers to seventeenth-century English political philosopher Thomas Hobbes.

21. R D Laing (1927-1989), Govanhill born psychiatrist, poet, writer and healer.

22. David Hume (1711-1776), Scottish philosopher, historian and somewhat closeted atheist. The paradoxical appears to have been important in Hume's methodology. For example the doubting of doubt; and the political paradox as pointed out by Noam Chomsky: "Hume said that power is always in the hands of the people who are oppressed - so how come they submit themselves to authority? Force is one element, but the real element is opinion. You have to control their opinion. Of course, [Hume] was in favour of it- he was a Tory..."

23. Fyodor Dostoyevsky (1821-1881), Russian novelist and writer whose short story 'Bobok' was first published in 1873.

24. Mikhail Bakhtin (1895-1975), Russian literary theorist and linguistic philosopher, his 'Problems of Dostoevsky's Poetics' was published in English in 1984.

25. John Wayne (1907-1979), Iconic Hollywood movie actor, politically right-wing in the mould of Ronald Reagan and Donald Trump.

26. Herbert Marcuse (1898-1979), Berlin born philosopher and political theorist. Author of 'One Dimensional Man' with some help from his

jim ferguson

wife.

27. Simone de Beauvoir (1908-1986) French novelist and philosopher, her novel 'The Mandarins' set at the end of World War 2 won the Prix Goncourt in 1954.

Jean Paul Sartre (1905-1980), French novelist and philosopher, sometime lover of de Beauvoir, his short story collection 'The Wall' was published in 1939 (first published in English in 1948 under the title 'Intimacy').

28. Woody Allen (b. 1935), Hollywood movie director, comedian and musician. His best known movie is probably 'Annie Hall' (1977).

29. 'The Glass Bead Game', novel by German writer Hermann Hesse (1877-1962), first published in 1943, first published in English in 1949.

30. Jean-Luc Goddard (b.1930), French-Swiss movie director. The movies that came to mind when writing this poem were 'Masculine-feminine' (1966) and 'Passion' (1982): both movies comment on the meaning of work. My enjoyment of Goddard was rekindled when I read the novel 'French Toast' by Peter Burnett.

31. Among the last words poet Tom Leonard (1944-2018) said to poet Jim Ferguson.

32. Henry Ford (1863-1947), American industrialist credited with the invention of the production line. Ford brought the mass produced automobile to ubiquity amongst humanity, held strongly anti-Semitic views. One may conjecture that being a fascist himself, Ford tried to distract people from the scent of his own fascism by claiming that Jews were responsible for Nazism in Germany. An example of what we now call 'victim blaming', possibly?

33. Mickey Rourke (b.1952), Hollywood movie actor, who according to some critics did not fulfil his potential.

34. Marlon Brando (1924-2004), Iconic Hollywood movie actor, who was active in the promotion of civil rights. Great performances include 'A Streetcar Named Desire' (1951),'On the Waterfront' (1954) and 'The Godfather' (1972) ; sings in 'Guys and Dolls' (1955).

35. John Struthers (1776-1853), East Kilbride born poet, songwriter, essayist and librarian. See, 'The Harp of Caledonia: a collection of songs, ancient and modern, chiefly Scottish. With an essay on Scottish song writers' (2 Vols. 1819, Glasgow).

36. Robert Tannahill (1774-1810), Paisley-born poet and songwriter: of whose poems and songs a twenty-first century edition is long overdue.

37. Graham Brodie (1970-2019), Edinburgh born poet.

38. Darth Vader, character of 'the dark-side' from the Hollywood movie 'Star Wars' (1977).

39. The Clash, English punk/post-punk rock band of the late 1970s and

early 1980s.

40. Isaac Newton (1643-1727), Physicist and Master of the Royal Mint. Best known for gravity.

41. 'Take back control' slogan used by brexiteers, allegedly invented by right-wing Conservative strategist Dominic Cummings.

42. Bob Dylan (b.1941), American singer-songwriter and Nobel Prize winner.

43. Thomas Moore (1779-1852), Irish poet, songwriter and satirist. On Saturday 2 December 1797 a letter written by Moore was published on the front page of the 'Press' which was a rallying cry for Ireland's liberty and freedom: "Ireland has sons untutored in the school of corruption, who love her Liberties, and, in the crisis, will die for them." Both Moore and Robert Emmet were students together at Trinity College, in the case of the latter this statement was to prove shockingly prophetic. See, Ronan Kelly, 'Bard of Erin: The Life of Thomas Moore', (Penguin, 2009) p.57.

44. James Cook (1728-1779), English sea captain, navigator and explorer. He discovered Australia. He was killed in Hawaii (in the same year Thomas Moore was born) after committing the ill-judged act of taking a Hawaiian leader hostage.

45. A reference to what has become known as 'The Windrush Scandal', it arose from a policy of creating a hostile environment for migrants and asylum seekers in the UK. A policy made explicit by Theresa May as British Home Secretary and remains in place at the time of writing (30 June 2020).

46. Robert Tannahill, Letter to James Clark, 20th September, 1807, (Glasgow University Library, Special Collections, MS Robertson, 1/9).

47. Francis Jeffrey (1773-1850), Edinburgh born editor of the 'Edinburgh Review' and Whig politician who was challenged to a duel with pistols by Thomas Moore.

48. Refers to the novel 'Steppenwolf' (1927: 1929 in English) by Hermann Hesse. See note 29.

49. The Bible, Matthew, 16:18.

50. Graham Fulton (b.1959), Born in Hampton, England, Fulton moved to Paisley, Scotland in 1963 and has dwelt there since, mostly. He is author of numerous books, mostly poetry.

51. Albert Camus (1913-1960), Algerian-French novelist, philosopher and essayist. Nobel prize winner. Killed in a car crash four days before Graham Fulton's first birthday.

52. Percy Bysshe Shelley (1792-1822), English radical poet: "Poets are the unacknowledged legislators of the World," he declared in his essay 'A Defence of Poetry'. John Struthers, sometime of the Gorbals,

jim ferguson

argued similarly of Scottish song in 'The Harp of Caledonia', which was published sometime before Shelley's essay.

53. Robert Tannahill, 'Epistle to Robert Allan', 14th March, 1808 (GUL, Spec Colls., MS Robertson 1/13).

54. Giambattista Vico (1668-1744), political philosopher and according to Sam Beckett "a practical roundheaded Neapolitan." Beckett, 'Disjecta', Grove Press, 1948. Jacques Lacan (1901-1981), French psychoanalyst and psychiatrist, not sure why he's in this to be honest!

55. Refers to English singer David Bowie's (1947-2016) Buddhist song, 'Silly Boy Blue'.

56. Refers to the song 'Au Suivant' written by Jacques Brel (1929-1978). Performed in English as 'Next' by Alex Harvey.

57. Refers to a poem by Percy Shelley.

58. A character from the board-game 'Cluedo'. A murder mystery game invented by Anthony E Pratt of Birmingham, England, in 1943. And also a Glasgow-based band 'Colonel Mustard and the Dijon 5'.

59. An English/UK institution which imposed its so-called Biblical moral values, particularly, on the poor.

60. Joseph Roth (1894-1939), Austrian novelist and journalist. See his story, 'The Cartel' written in 1923, in 'Collected Shorter Fiction of Joseph Roth', London, 2001.

61. Hannah Arendt (1906-1975), German political philosopher; like G Vico she mistrusted Cartesianism.

62. 'Betty Blue' (1986), a French movie directed by Jean-Jacques Beineix. A paraphrase from a speech by John F Kennedy.

63. Zadie Smith (b.1975), English novelist and essayist.

ALSO FROM RYMOUR BOOKS

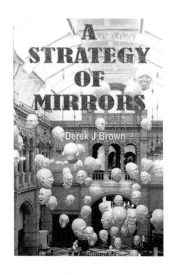

Derek J Brown
A Strategy of Mirrors
142pp, 213x135mm, RRP £9.90

'This collection expresses exactly the kind of vision I seek in the poetry I read, an understanding acquired past the limits of exhaustion, a knowledge that turns metaphysics into a childish toy'. PETER CLIVE